INVASION ALERT!

# INVASION OF THE BURMESE PYTHON

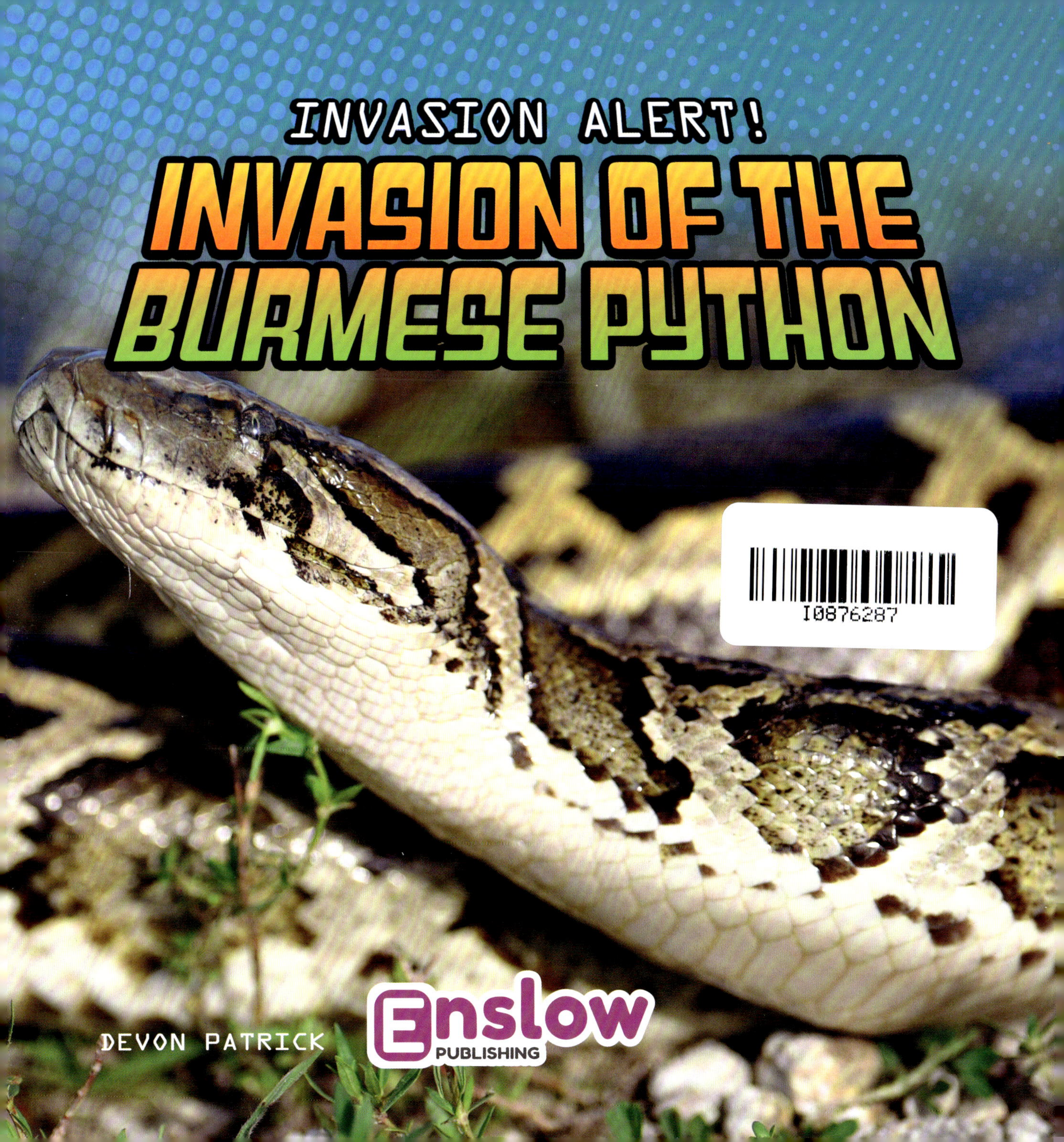



DEVON PATRICK

Enslow PUBLISHING

Please visit our website, www.enslow.com. For a free color catalog of all our high-quality books, call toll free 1-800-398-2504 or fax 1-877-980-4454



Published in 2027 by
**Enslow Publishing**
2544 Clinton Street
Buffalo, NY 14224



Portions of this work were originally authored by Matthew Jankowski and published as *Animal Invaders: Destroying Native Habitats: Attack of the Burmese Pythons.* All new material in this edition is authored by Devon Patrick.



Cataloging-in-Publication Data
Names: Patrick, Devon.
Title: Invasion of the Burmese python / Devon Patrick.
Description: Buffalo, NY : Enslow Publishing, 2027. | Series: Invasion alert! | Includes glossary and index.
Identifiers: ISBN 9781978548367 (pbk.) | ISBN 9781978548374 (library bound) | ISBN 9781978548381 (ebook)
Subjects: LCSH: Burmese python--Juvenile literature. | Introduced reptiles--Juvenile literature. | Pest introduction--Juvenile literature.
Classification: LCC QL666.O63 D486 2027 | DDC 597.9678--dc23

Printed in China

Photos Credits: Cover, p. 1, 11 Florida Fish and Wildlife Conservation Commission; cover, p. 1, 3, 4, 6, 8, 10, 12, 14, 16, 18, 20, 22, 23, 24 (dot pattern) Nurin Nabila A/Shutterstock.com; p. 4, 6, 8, 10, 12, 14, 16, 18, 20 (sidebar frame) HST6/Shutterstock.com; p. 4 CK2 Connect Studio/Shutterstock.com; p. 5 Gulliver20/Shutterstock.com; p. 7 LesPalenik/Shutterstock.com; p. 9 Wikipedia; p. 9 John Apte/Shutterstock.com; p. 13 Paul Tessier/Shutterstock.com; p. 15 ISHOWCAM/Shutterstock.com; p. 17 Paramonov Alexander/Shutterstock.com; p. 19 SunflowerMomma/Shutterstock.com; p. 21 Mr. Kosal/Shutterstock.com

CPSIA compliance information: Batch #QSENS27: For further information, contact Enslow Publishing, New York, New York, at 1-800-398-2504.

# CONTENTS



Words in the glossary appear in **bold** type the first time they are used in the text.

# SLITHERING SNAKES

Are you afraid of snakes? Some people are! Snakebites can be painful, and some can even be deadly. Not all snakes are dangerous to people, but even snakes that don't bite can be a problem.

Burmese pythons are one species, or kind, of snake causing trouble in the United States. That's because they're an invasive species in southern Florida. Invasive species make homes in areas far from their natural **habitats**. They can be harmful to native animals and plants and are often difficult to control.

### STAY ALERT

Burmese pythons don't chew their **prey**. They swallow it whole!

*Like all pythons, Burmese pythons are constrictors. This means that they kill the animals they eat by constricting, or squeezing, them until they're unable to breathe.*

# MEET THE BURMESE PYTHON

Burmese pythons are native to parts of Southeast Asia, including India, China, Myanmar, and many islands nearby. They commonly live in rainforests near streams but can live in other habitats as long as there's water close by. Burmese pythons are cold-blooded, which means their body heat changes to match their surroundings. They need a warm environment to survive.

Burmese pythons were brought to North America in the 1970s as exotic pets. Thousands of pet snakes were sold in Florida in the 1980s.

**STAY ALERT**

Burmese pythons can grow to be very large. Their bodies are as thick as a telephone pole and can be more than 20 feet (6 m) long!

*Many people have cats, dogs, and fish as pets, but some people have pet snakes. Burmese pythons became popular pets because they were thought to be* ***docile****.*

# BURMESE PYTHON TAKEOVER

Many owners couldn't handle their pet snakes after they got too big, so they released them into the swamps of the Florida Everglades. The weather in southern Florida is a lot like Burmese pythons' native Asia, so it was easy for them to make a home in the wild there. The pythons have plenty of prey, including birds, squirrels, deer—and even alligators!

Now, Burmese pythons are one of the most damaging invasive species that the Florida Everglades has ever seen. The area is getting overrun.

**STAY ALERT**

It's possible that some Burmese pythons escaped from a **breeding** facility in southern Florida that was destroyed in a hurricane.

The Florida Everglades is a large area of swampland in south Florida. It's bigger than the entire state of Rhode Island!

# SUPERSIZED SNAKES

Burmese pythons are one of the biggest species of snakes in the world. They can grow to be 23 feet (7 m) long and weigh up to 200 pounds (90 kg). Picture that in your bedroom and you can see how they are too big to be pets!

Burmese pythons can swim, burrow, and climb trees. They have sharp teeth that curve backward, but they don't use them to chew. Instead, they use their teeth to hold prey and stop it from escaping as it's squeezed to death. Then, they swallow their prey whole.

### STAY ALERT

Burmese pythons will eat almost anything, including large animals. In 2024, scientists saw a Burmese python swallowing a whole deer.

Burmese pythons are light brown with dark brown splotches on their scaly skin. These spots help them blend in with their surroundings.

# MOTHERS AND BABIES

Like many snakes, Burmese pythons lay eggs. Once a year, female Burmese pythons lay a clutch, or group, of about 35 eggs. Some can even lay more than 100 eggs at a time!

Baby pythons hatch, or come out of, their eggs by using a special egg tooth to cut their way out. But once they hatch, they're on their own. Their mother leaves, and they have to teach themselves how to hunt for food and watch out for **predators**. Burmese pythons can live about 30 years in the wild.

### STAY ALERT

Young Burmese pythons spend time in trees, but as they grow, they tend to stay on the ground. That's because trees are no longer strong enough to hold them!

*Female Burmese pythons coil their body around their eggs to **incubate** them. The eggs' shells are leathery and soft, and feel like they're filled with jelly.*

# HOME IN THE EVERGLADES

Everglades National Park has become the Burmese pythons' new home in Florida. Today, there are thousands of these snakes found in this one wetland. Scientists don't know the exact number, but it could be up to 300,000!

The Burmese python is a huge risk to the Everglades **ecosystem**. Its only predators in the Everglades are alligators and people. Nothing else is large enough to kill it! As the Burmese python continues to spread, native predator and prey **relationships** are thrown out of balance.

### STAY ALERT

Despite their numbers, visitors to the Everglades probably won't see any Burmese pythons. They're great at hiding and blending in, which makes them difficult for scientists to count.

Without predators to stop them, Burmese python populations are increasing rapidly.

# TOUGH COMPETITION

Burmese pythons compete with native snakes for food and living space—and often win! Native snakes are getting pushed out of their home.

Burmese pythons have many babies and live a long time, which means there are a lot of them. They also grow much larger than any of Florida's native snakes. The indigo snake, which is the second largest snake in the area, only grows to be less than half the size of a Burmese python.

### STAY ALERT

Since Burmese pythons were introduced to the Florida Everglades, the number of **mammals** there has decreased. Small animals like rabbits and foxes have mostly disappeared.

The Everglades is home to many **endangered** species, some of which have become prey for the Burmese python.

# ON THE MOVE

Burmese pythons can **adapt** to live in many kinds of habitats. They have already begun spreading beyond the Everglades to other parts of Florida. Scientists are worried they'll become invasive species in other **vulnerable** ecosystems, such as the Florida Keys. In fact, they've already been found on Key Largo!

The spread of this snake isn't good news for people, either. Despite being kept as pets, Burmese pythons can hurt people. Luckily, serious attacks are very rare.

**STAY ALERT**

Burmese pythons are now an established species in some parts of Florida. This means there are many of them living and breeding in an area.

Burmese pythons are excellent swimmers. They can stay underwater for up to 30 minutes before coming up for air.

# STOP THOSE SNAKES!

Controlling the Burmese python spread isn't easy. People are being taught how to spot and report the snakes so they can be caught. Some Burmese pythons are even being tracked, in the hope that they might lead the way to more snakes!

Some fear the Burmese python will spread to more parts of the United States, as the snakes have already been found moving north. Others see the problems in Florida, but don't think the snakes will go too far. When will the Burmese python invasion end?

**STAY ALERT**

Some scientists studied if people are good at spotting snakes in the wilderness. It turns out that humans only see them 1 percent of the time. Snakes are great at hiding!

South Florida gets quite hot, especially during the summer months. Burmese pythons are more active at night, when temperatures are cooler.

# GLOSSARY

**adapt:** to change to suit conditions

**breed:** to mate two animals so they produce others like them. Also, when two animals mate.

**docile:** easily taught, led, or controlled

**ecosystem:** all the living things in an area

**endangered:** in danger of dying out

**habitat:** the natural place where an animal or plant lives

**incubate:** to keep eggs warm so they can hatch

**mammals:** a warm-blooded animal that has hair or fur and usually gives birth to live babies

**predator:** an animal that hunts other animals for food

**prey:** an animal that is hunted by other animals for food

**relationship:** a connection between two things, animals, or people

**vulnerable:** able to be harmed

# FACT CHECK

1. Burmese pythons are______________, which means their body heat changes to match their surroundings.
   a. warm-blooded b. cold-blooded c. exotic

2. Female Burmese pythons lay a ____________ of about 35 eggs.
   a. coil b. burrow c. clutch

3. True or false: Burmese pythons use their teeth to chew their food.
   a. true b. false

Answers: 1. b, 2. c, 3. b

# ON THE INTERNET

**Burmese Python**

*https://kids.nationalgeographic.com/animals/reptiles/facts/burmese-python*

Learn more about these invasive snakes and watch a short video about Burmese pythons in the Everglades.

**Burmese Python Facts for Kids**

*https://kids.kiddle.co/Burmese_python*

Read all about these large snakes and see a map of where they've been spotted in the United States.

**Publisher's note to educators and parents:** Our editors have carefully reviewed these websites to ensure that they are suitable for students. Many websites change frequently, however, and we cannot guarantee that a site's future contents will continue to meet our high standards of quality and educational value. Be advised that students should be closely supervised whenever they access the Internet.

# INDEX